Live Like Dragons

poems by
Jeffrey-Paul Horn

Clare Songbirds Publishing House Chapbook Series
ISBN 978-1-947653-02-3
Clare Songbirds Publishing House
Live Like Dragons © 2017 Jeffrey-Paul Horn
All Rights Reserved. Clare Songbirds Publishing House retains right to reprint.
Permission to reprint individual poems must be obtained from the author who owns the copyright.

Printed in the United States of America
FIRST EDITION

Clare Songbirds Publishing House Mission Statement: Clare Songbirds Publishing House was established to provide a print forum for the creation of limited edition, fine art from poets and writers, both established and emerging. We strive to reignite and continue a tradition of quality, accessible literary arts to the national and international community of writers, and readers. We support our literary artists with high quality services and on-going support. Chapbook manuscripts and art quality poetry broadsides are carefully chosen for their ability to propel the expansion of art and ideas in literary form. We provide an accessible way to promote the art of words in order to resonate with, and impact, readers not yet familiar with the siren song of poets and writers. Clare Songbirds Publishing House espouses a singular cultural development where poetry creates community and becomes common-place in public places.

Clare Songbirds Publishing House
140 Cottage Street
Auburn, New York 13021
www.ClareSongbirdspub.com

Contents

Live, Love and Laughter	5
Wise Woman	6
Survivors Lament	7
Only Shadows	8
Follow Me	10
The Struggle	11
A Jack…	12
T.V.	13
Ode to My Hometown	14
Worn From Past Torments	16
Austin	17
I am a Man	18
Haiku #27	20
Dragon's Breath	22
Live Like Dragons	23

Life, Love and Laughter

Life is but a melody
a dream lost to sleep
a steady beat
brought by the earths rhythms
Life is a constant voyage
an open passage
to the wide open fields of wisdom
Love
a fickle emotion
to disrupt life's meaning
beautiful yet random
Laughter is life's elixir
a natural suppressant to pain
magical potent power
to forget life's burdens
Laugh and love
and embrace it's creations
for one day it will all be over

Wise Woman

A wise woman died in vain yesterday
She stared at a town lost in dismay

Her words falling only upon deaf and useless ears

Her eyes staring back cry only for help
wanting desperately
to be escorted gently back down her corridors
of lost euphoria

Tapping into the currents of life
and leaving only false pretense

Frustration pours out her bodily cortex
birthing creatures of pure ridicule
hungry for any ounce of ill-gotten emotion

Stealing the sanity
from a whole town of struggling dissidents

Survivors Lament

I'll hail a cab over by the light
and let's never speak again of what we did tonight
Two more beans and one more vike
no more coke, You're fried tonight
Just wait right here, we'll be moving soon
Don't get caught in the light of the moon
Ignore the sounds of the crooner's croon
and the music man playing so out of tune
I'll stand here and just face the wall
because I cant stand to see you fall
I'm glad you don't fear the constant call
but your going away effects us all

Only Shadows

They danced in murky distance
while we watched their lustful silhouettes

They gave us hope for love
until they fell
leaving only shadows

Whether in cool dark autumn
or in crisp warm spring
we wake with visions of a new horizon
looking out with muted exuberance
when we realize the night has left
only shadows

In her wake
on long hard trails
after painful losses
with my heart in stitch
I see only shadows

Behind me
when she reaches for my hand
through dim fog
and darker plight
she sees only shadows

These shadows of a past
cast from the light of lost love
haunt our every nightmare

Memories have no meaning now
if they're shared with her

Time is just a paradox
lost in these cool dark shadows

I thought I could love
in the center of the sun

I thought I could light the way
no matter where we'd run

I saw through times of agony
I am a stranger to the light

I am a man of only dreams
I am a stranger to sight

Now you love me in day's full bloom
in passionate nights lit by the moon

But inevitable darkness will surely come
when all is said and the light is none

I will fade with the light of the sun
for I am no man, no mortal son

I
am a shadow

Follow Me

I bebop along freely
never yielding in the mind's traf-
fic
It is for you
I incessantly fiend
yet never find
never mind
I'm not trying
but I'm yearning

searching
waiting
loving

seeing
Seeing my time as my leader
my conscious
and my fate

That's why I just cant wait
to find my way to freedoms gate

To let you see my misery

So follow me my golden key
to that far away shanty of souls

Follow me lustfully
follow me to the end

The Struggle

Still struggling
smile on my face
though that's a struggle too

Eatin' scraps now
no liquor
no bullion
no hot apple pies

No ladies to love
though plenty of flies

Got expensive gin dreams
and a heart that's wide open

I remain frail
while I remain here

Seems I've got plenty to hide
but little to fear

A Jack took the Queens Ace
and her King's face was Red
The diamonds laughed but the Clubs cried
for all the Hearts were dead

So the knowing masses gathered
still eating what they were fed
Then all were silent and stood aside
when they saw a Joker led

T.V.

The Boxes fodder fills the dimly lit room
haunted with the realization of broken
dreams

Doubt echoes in one's mind
as he trudges on divided

He's between dreams and reality
becoming the predator of his own fate
tearing himself limb from limb from within

Ode To My Hometown

Empty, shallow, nothing, damn
kiss my ass you greedy pigs

covered in shit
reeking of hate

I love but in hate I live

Hotel rooms and airplanes
take me to that familiar place

In asteroid skies
the crimson tides
running through a dreamers mind

Instead there's infest
rat poison candy bars
golden brown murder

Take it all in my friend
my witness to the end
Likely to be the advocate of death
the bearer of poison lust

Dead to the touch
blind to the truth
and ignorant youths

The smell of trash mongers fill the air

Tension

So bow your heads to these headstones
burials and lipstick blowjobs

Bow your head for me

For I am trapped with no escape

A child scared
Yet without a care I wander these lonely streets
another animal

135 more pounds of prey

Worn From Past Torments

Worn from past torments,
I stand alone and weak.
Weighed down by heavy tears in lustlorn eyes.
I find myself in vast dissolution
surrounded only by madness and the past
as voices and memories of childhood passions
fill my weary sorrows.
Feed me your heart-felt splendor.
Let me carry in your wind
as I feel the soft touch of your warm delicate hands,
I beg you.
My voice rasped from lonesome screams,
Don't you hear me?
It is you I am reaching to.
Hold me in your flawless surrender,
treasure my touch as I do yours.
Give my tattered body refuge from the pain.
This pain that eats me entirely from the inside out.
Shelter me from the demons
that prey upon my emotional frailty.
My insecurity runs amiss in your golden garden of beauty
because I am the lesser you.
Do you see me?
In my cold and
broken world of disarray.

AUSTIN

I feel the city
-Lost

It is alive inside

I feel the music

the spastic space beats
moving the losers
to winners rhythms

If only for one night

I'm down to 22 cents

I need a beer

Awash with anxiety

and I need a beer

Uncertainty presents itself as kin
I'm dwindling

Hanging on by a thin fucking thread

Tied to the same spears
that impale my sanity

I Am a Man

I am a man
entrapped in my own prison of virtue

of needs unneeded
wants unwanted

I pass the paupers
and hide my envy

Their freedom is indelible

A stolen bastion of bucolic buffoonery
wrapped inside disorder

Pork and bean fantasies
of train trodden enigmas
run through my mind in dreams

midnight marauders

Made in moonlit memories
of Sisco and Sonny

Sung about in folk tunes
haunt my aspirational motivations

I'm more than moved to
make way for maniacal journeys
into the sun or sea

over roadways of gold

away from the risen morays
and into the benevolent bosom

of a mother unknown

Haiku # 27

Outside the leaves flutter
and dance in the cold harsh wind
as do we in life

Dragon's Breath

The sun is a dragon's breath
Life is a lie

We float dumb and dying all the time

Fat mouths eat freedom

Small minds bleed truth

End

Live Like Dragons
a poem about humanity

Live like dragons
and kill like kings
Soar
with stolen angel's wings

Let's live like dragons
in freedoms fire
in moonlit lands
of muck and mire

I am a dragon
a sinner's saint
Pitch fork in Eden's garden
a snake in wait

www.ingramcontent.com/pod-product-compliance
Lightning Source LLC
Chambersburg PA
CBHW062041120526
44592CB00035B/1830